PROVERBS & SAYINGS OF IRELAND

The words of the wise and their dark sayings
(Book of Proverbs)

The proverb cannot be bettered
(Irish Proverb)

When a fool is told a proverb, its meaning has to be
explained to him
(Ashanti Proverb)

PROVERBS & SAYINGS OF IRELAND

Edited by
Sean Gaffney & Seamus Cashman

Proverbs & Sayings of Ireland

Edition 1985
First published 1974
Paperback editions 1976, 1978, 1979, 1982
© 1974 Wolfhound Press

ISBN 0 9503454 0 7
ISBN 0 9503454 4 X (Paperback)

CONTENTS

25 illustrations by Billy Merwick

ACKNOWLEDGEMENTS

We acknowledge with gratitude the contributions and encouragement of many friends, in particular our parents, Ann and James Cashman, and Margaret Gaffney. A special word of thanks to Margaret Ryan, Deirdre Duffy, Monica Miller, Joy Adams, John Logue and Paul Walsh.

CLASSIFICATIONS

Ability
Advice
Affectation
Age
Anger
Appearance
Art
As....as...
Beauty
Betrayer
Bitterness
Blessings
Boasting
Borrowing
Bravery
Bribery
Carelessness
Caution
Change
Character
Charity
Chastity
Children
Choice
Clergy
Coincidence
Comfort
Compromise
Contentment
Conversation
Courtship
Criticism
Cunning
Curses
Cynicism
Danger
Death

Debt
Deception
Delusion
Desire
Despair
Devil
Discipline
Dismissal
Drink
Economy
Education
Effort
Egotism
Eloquence
Endurance
English, The
Equality
Error
Evil
Excused
Experience
Fair-haired
Fame
Familiarity
Fate
Fear
Fighting
Flattery
Flimsiness
Food
Fool
Foolishness
Forgiveness
Fortune
Frail
Freedom
Friendship

Futility
Gambling
Generosity
Gentleness
God
Goodness
Gossip
Gratitude
Greed
Grief
Happiness
Health
Home
Honesty
Honour
Hope
Humility
Humour
Hunger
Idleness
Ignorance
Impossibility
Independence
Inequality
Initiative
Intelligence
Involvement
Irishman
Judgement
Justice
Kerry
Kindness
Kinship
Knowledge
Law
Laziness
Leadership

CLASSIFICATIONS

Lies
Life
Love
Luck
Manners
Marriage
Maturity
Meanness
Men
Misfortune
Mother
Nature
Neatness
Necessity
Nobility
Obedience
Obligation
Ownership
Participation
Patience
Patriotism
Peace
Perception
Pity
Poetry
Possession
Poverty
Power
Presumption
Pride
Procrastination
Promise
Proverbs
Prudence
Red-hair
Repentance
Reputation

Revenge
Rogue
Rumour
Scarcity
Seasons
Secret
Self-destruction
Selfishness
Sense
Separation
Shame
Shyness
Silence
Strength
Stupidity
Success
Suitability
Tact
Talent
Talkativeness
Thrift
Time
Treachery
Trouble
Trust
Truth
Understanding
Uselessness
Value
Vanity
Warning
Wastefulness
Wealth
Weather
Welcome
Widow
Wisdom

Women
Work
Youth

INTRODUCTION

'The proverb cannot be bettered'; 'though the proverb is abandoned, it cannot be falsified'. How true these are the reader will best discover for himself in the following collection of Irish proverbs, sayings and triads. The triad is perhaps the most fascinating type of saying and though little heard today in the non-Irish speaking parts of the country, it is still to be heard in the Gaeltacht areas, especially in West Cork, West Galway and the Aran Islands.

A glance through the index of key words reveals the range of the Irish proverb, its themes, and the imagery and symbols used. As might be expected, the reputed vulnerability of our race to religion and romanticism is well represented. But the story the proverb tells is not quite that of a priest-ridden peasantry content in their poverty. Rather it shows us to have — or at least to have had — a subtle, sly perhaps, but generally humorous self-confidence. 'The priest's pig' may get 'the most porridge'; but the proverb also advises us to be 'neither intimate nor distant with the clergy'! Nor are we shown to be wholly susceptible to romanticism: 'it's better to be lucky than to be an early riser' but 'there's no success without authority and laws'. The proverbs reveal a deep conviction in a relationship between the spiritual and the material that is both challenging and realistic.

Proverbs are, in a sense, a race's unconscious expression of its moral attitudes. Our proverbs seem frequently to take the form of a national confession of sins: the evils of drink, gambling, greed, vanity, improvidence abound. But the virtues are there: faith, gentleness, love of nature, tolerance, and a trust in a life after death that offers a constant check to the materialism already mentioned.

Irish proverbs are rich in nature symbolism and imagery: the wind, the sea, the mountains; plants, animals, birds and fishes. The kingfisher, mackerel, thistle, plover, the horse and the hare, even the common crow are all called upon to mirror our achievements, hopes and failings.

While the proverbs of a race are often readily identifiable as belonging to that race, the ideas expressed and the images used touch on matters more fundamental than a national identity. One can readily accept that Irish proverbs should have their exact counterparts among the proverbs of other Celtic races. There are numerous examples of similarities among the sayings of the Irish, Welsh and Scottish — A long illness doesn't lie (Irish); To be long sick and to die nevertheless (Welsh); Marriage at the dungheap and the Godparents far away (Irish); Marriage o'er the anvil, sponsorship o'er the sea (Scottish); A drink is shorter than a story (Irish and Manx); Bribery splits a stone (Irish); Envy splits a stone (Scottish). Such typical proverbs as these listed here also have their counterparts in most European languages.

However, it is interesting to discover that our proverbs also have affinities with those of races as far distant as the West Indies and Africa. Among Jamaican blacks, who are of African descent, there is a saying: 'When you sleep wid darg, you ketch him flea'. Our equivalent is: 'He who lies with dogs rises with fleas'. We speak of sending the goose on a message to the foxes' den; the Hausa of West Africa have: 'Even if the hyena's town is destroyed, one does not send a dog in to trade'.

Irish proverbs and saying derive from two mainstreams: the gaelic tradition, in the Irish language, and the anglo-Irish tradition, in the English language. Both reflect the strong biblical influence found in the proverbs throughout 'western' countries. This collection includes some of the oldest seanfhocail (old-sayings) recorded in Ireland as well as sayings of more recent origin. But it is by no means exhaustive. The exact origins of most of these sayings are unknown: perhaps a throw-away phrase; perhaps a line of a poem long forgotten - who knows? It is what survives that matters.

For readers interested in pursuing the Irish Proverb further, a brief word on some sources. Several substantial collections have been published (from which many in this collection have been taken, and which we gratefully acknowledge.) Most of these are unfortunately long out of print. The most recent, and certainly the finest is T. S. O'Maille, ed., *Sean-fhocala Chonnacht,* 2 vols. (Dublin, 1948-52). Others are: T. O'Donoghue, ed., *Sean-fhocail na Mumhain,* a Gaelic League publication, 1902; E. Ua Muirgheasa, ed., *Sean fhocla Uladh,* (1907) which contains English translations as does T. F. O'Rahilly, *A Miscellany of Irish Proverbs,* (Dublin, 1922). Shorter collections will be found in J. O'Daly, *Irish Language Miscellany,* Burke, *Irish Grammar;* Hardiman, *Irish Minstrelsy,* 2 vols. reissued by IUP in 1969; the *Gaelic Journal* and *The Ulster Journal of Archaeology.* P. W. Joyce, *English as we Speak it in Ireland,* (Dublin, 1910) is a useful and entertaining starting point though of limited use for proverbs. Two important sources still to be fully researched are the Douglas Hyde 'Diaries' in the National Library of Ireland, and the manuscript collections of the Irish Folklore Department in UCD, in particular the 'Schools Mss.' for anglo-Irish proverbs. *Bealoideas* the journal of the Folklore Commission includes lists of proverbs in its various issues. Information on further sources will be found in bibliographies in the published works mentioned.

Most of the proverbs in this collection have been translated from the Irish language. English translations of proverbs in the Irish language are not always successful. We have endeavoured to remain as close to the original as possible. An illustration of the effects of translation, however, can be readily seen by comparing 'One beetle recognises another' with the original Irish proverb 'Aithnionn ciarog ciarog eile'. The impact of the expression depends greatly on the sound of the word ciarog, and its repetition. The pattern cannot be reproduced satisfactorily in English; and the word 'beetle' is by comparison with the Irish word, weak and ineffectual.

We have classified each proverb by subject recognising that such classification is both limiting and subjective. For proverbs are by their very nature elusive and usually defy adequate classification under any one heading. However as the index contains the key-words of each proverb, our arrangement should cause the reader little difficulty.

PROVERBS & SAYINGS OF IRELAND

PROVERBS & SAYINGS OF IRELAND

Ability

No one can tell what he is able to do till he tries   1

You can't whistle and chew meal at the same time   2

You can't bark and run at the same time   3

A vessel only holds its fill   4

Often the hound that was made fun of killed the deer   5

The strong man may when he wants to; the weak
     man when he's able   6

The gobadan (kingfisher) cannot work both tides   7

Advice

Don't give cherries to pigs; don't give advice to a fool   8

A man is often a bad adviser to himself and a good
     adviser to another   9

The man who won't have advice will have conflict   10

He is bad that will not take advice, but he is a
     thousand times worse that takes every advice   11

The cat is his own best adviser   11a

Crafty advice is often got from a fool   12

A wise man takes advice   13

Affectation

A ring on her finger and not a stitch of clothes
     on her back   14

Sparing at home and lavish in the hospital   15

Like the sun on the hill-top, but like a thistle
     on the hearth   16

Street angel, house devil   17

PROVERBS & SAYINGS OF IRELAND

Age

Anger

Appearance

Art

As...

   A localised Kerry expression. When the Irish
   were being hunted down in Penal times a
   particularly vicious duo, a Captain Barrington
   and Colonel Nelson used a bloodhound to chase
   their quarry which savaged the victim terribly,
   hence giving rise to the saying.

   A Cork expression. The story goes that the goat
   belonged to Atwell Hayes who was father of
   Sir Henry Hayes, sherrif of Cork in 1790. The
   goat was reputed to be old even when Atty was
   a young man. A generation later Captain Philip
   Allen, son-in-law of Sir Henry Hayes became
   mayor of Cork, (in 1800) and gave a civil
   banquet to celebrate the occasion. At this time
   the goat died and Allen being a bit of a joker
   served up the hind quarters of the goat
   unknowingly to his guests, as venison. The
   'venison' was proclaimed by the city fathers as
   delicious. In county Armagh the corresponding
   expression is 'As old as Killylea bog'.

As wise as the women of Mungret 45
A Limerick expression. The very amusing story attached to this saying concerns the monastic foundation and school at Mungret. A number of scholars was sent from Cashel to compete with their Mungret counterparts. However the Limerick scholars fearing defeat and the loss of their reputation dressed as washerwomen and waited along the roadside, washing in the nearby river. As the Cashel contingent approached and asked the 'women' for directions they were completely taken aback when answered in perfect Greek. Thinking that if the washerwomen were so learned then the scholars must be unusually brilliant, the poor Tipperary monks turned for home, leaving the reputation of Mungret intact and untarnished!

As hard as the hob of hell 46

As cunning as the fox 47

As long as a wet Sunday 48

As old as the hills 49

As bald as a buailtin *(see notes)* 50

As sharp as a ciotog *(see notes)* 51

As bitter as thick milk 52

As crooked as a ram's horn 53

As brown as a berry 54

As big as a smith's meitheal *(see notes)* 55

As sharp as the word of a fool 56

As sharp as the teeth of a hound 57

As wet as dung 58

As pretty as a May flower 59

As old as the Cailleach Beare *(see notes)* 60

As fresh as a daisy 61

As bright as a lily 62

As slow as a late dinner   63

As dull as ditchwater   64

As swift as a hare   65

As true as the gospel   66

As deep as the sea   67

As bashful as a girl   68

As treacherous as an Englishman   69

As melodious as a lark   70

As brave as Fionn MacCumhall *(see notes)*   71

As yellow as a ragweed (ragworth)   72

As lazy as a donkey   73

As lazy as a piper's luidin (little finger)   73a

As busy as a bee   74

As salty as the sea   75

As good as gold   76

As rich as Damer   77
  A Dublin expression, not in common usage.
  The story is based on Joseph Damer who was
  born in 1630. After serving Cromwell he
  returned to Ireland where he purchased much
  land forfeited in the Williamite confiscations.
  He became a banker and achieved much
  notoriety as a miser. He died in 1720 leaving
  nearly half a million pounds, a phenomenal
  amount even by to-day's standards. Jonathan
  Swift was moved, as was his wont, to comment
  unfavourably on Mr. Damer:
  The ghost of old Damer who left not his betters
  When it heard of a bank appear'd to his debtors
  And lent them for money the backs of his letters
  His debtors they wonder'd to find him so frank,
  For old Nick gave the papers the mark of the bank.

As hairy as a puck-goat's head   77a

As thieving as a fox's snout   77b

PROVERBS & SAYINGS OF IRELAND

Beauty

Betrayer

Bitterness

Blessings

May I see you in heaven	95
God bless three times, and three spits for luck (said at the birth of a calf)	95a

Boasting

There are two heads on all his sheep	96

Borrowing

The law of borrowing is to break the borrower	97
The borrowed horse has hard hoofs	98
The loan of something on loan	99
Don't exchange your horse when you are crossing the river	100
He who is bad to give the loan is good for directing you	101

Bravery

The brave man never loses	102
Every dog is valiant at his own door	103
Every hound is brave on his own dunghill	104
Every man is bold until he faces a crowd	105

Bribery

Bribe the rogue and you need have no fear of the honest man	106
Beware of the bribed man	107
Bribery will split a stone	108
Hold on to the bone and the dog will follow you	109

Carelessness

Caution

Change

Character

Charity

Chastity

Children

Choice

Clergy

Criticism

A good horseman is the man on the ground	192
He's a good hurler that's on the ditch	193
The one who loses the game has the liberty of talking	194

Cunning

He would cover a rock with hay and sell it for a haycock	195
He would skin a louse and send the hide and fat to market	196
He would build a nest in your ear	197
In spite of the fox's cunning, his skin is often sold	198
He'd steal the cross of an ass's back	199
He would steal the egg from the crane and finally the crane herself	200
Cunning is better than strength	201

Curses

The curse does not fall on a stick or a stone	202
A bad death to you	203
Bad cess to you *(see notes)*	203a
A heart-burning on you	204
A cold day on you	205
The raven's curse on you	206
The kitten's death to you	207
May your trouble be in your throat	208
The curse of Cromwell on you	208a

Cynicism

PROVERBS & SAYINGS OF IRELAND

Danger

Death

Debt

Deception

Delusion

Excuses

Experience

Fair-haired

If I am yellow I have a fair heart   318

Fame

Fame lasts longer than life   319
Without money fame is dead   320
Falling is easier than rising   321
Greatness knows modesty   322

Familiarity

To know somebody, (one must) live in the same
    house with him   323
Too much of one thing is the same as nothing   324
Familiarity breeds contempt   325
People of the same trade are friendly   326

Fate

Long as the day may be the night comes at last   327
He that is born to be hanged needn't fear water   328
Every nursling as it is nursed, every web as it is
    woven   329
Pity the man drowned in the storm; for after
    the rain comes the sunshine   330
The darkest hour is nearest dawn   331
A ship is often lost by the harbour   332
No matter how often a pitcher goes to the water,
    it is broken in the end   333
No matter how long the day, night comes   334

What kills one man gives life to another 335

About the foot of the tree the foliage falls 336

Fear

Fear is a fine spur, so is rage 337

Be afraid, and you'll not meet danger 338

The man who is struck on the head, will
    afterwards be afraid 339

Fighting

To fight like Kilkenny cats 340
    In 1798 when the Hessians were quartered
in Kilkenny they amused themselves by tying
two cats tails together and throwing them over
a line, to fight. Their officer on hearing of this,
ordered his men to stop. However the soldiers
continued the practice in secret, and one day
while they were amusing themselves in this
manner they heard the officer approaching.
One soldier drawing his sword cut down the
cats leaving only their tails hanging. When the
officer enquired as to where the cats were, the
soldier replied that the cats had fought so
furiously that they had devoured all but each
other's tails. The story proved immensely
popular and achieved widespread fame, but it
is probably just a tall tale!

Quarrelsome dogs get dirty coats 341

Don't kick till you're spurred 342

Be warning but not striking 343

A word goes to the wind but a blow goes to the
    bones 344

Wine is better than blood 345

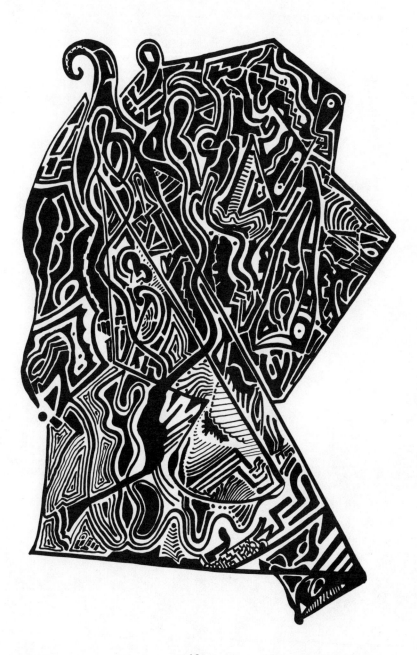

Foolishness

Forgiveness

Fortune

The lucky man awaits prosperity, the unlucky man gives a blind leap   380

Let each person judge his own luck, good or bad   381

Frail

The point of a rush would draw blood from his cheek   382

Freedom

Let every man have his own world   383

You can take the horse to the well, but you can't make him drink   384

Friendship

No war is as bitter as a war between friends, but it doesn't last long   385

Reverence ceases once blood is spilled   386

Two persons never lit a fire without disagreeing   387

If you will walk with lame men you will soon limp yourself   388

There was never a scabby sheep in a flock that didn't like to have a comrade   389

The man long absent is forgotten   390

In times of trouble friends are recognised   391

A friend's eye is a good mirror   392

Reckoning up is the ending of friendship   393

The friend that can be bought is not worth buying   394

If I like the sow I like her litter   395

Futility

Gambling

Generosity

Gentleness

God

Goodness

Gossip

PROVERBS & SAYINGS OF IRELAND

Gratitude

Greed

Grief

There is no cure for grief but to put it under
    your foot   489

Happiness

There is no happiness without an inch of sorrow
through it   490

Health

The herb that can't be got is the one that brings
relief   491

A good laugh and a long sleep, the best cures
in a doctor's book   492

Sickness is the physician's feast   493

The beginning of a ship is a board, of a kiln a
stone, of a king's reign salutation, and the
beginning of health is sleep   494

A long disease doesn't tell a lie; it kills at last   495

Health is better than wealth   496

Health is better than flocks   497

A healthy man is a king   498

The relapse is worse than the final fever   499

Every patient is a doctor after his own cure   500

What butter or whiskey will not cure, there's
no cure for   501

A long illness doesn't lie   502

Beginning with a cough and ending with a coffin   503

A graveyard cough   504

The person who doesn't scatter the morning
dew will not comb grey hairs   505

One must pay health its tithes   506

The physician's hope, every misfortune   507

Patience is the cure for an old illness   508

Home

There is no fireside like your own fireside	509
It's a long way from home that the plover cries	509a

Honesty

When rogues disagree, honest men get their own	510
The man that steals stacks thinks all the world thieves	511
The miller's pigs are fat but God knows whose meal they ate	512
He is as honest as the priest	513

Honour

A patch is better than a hole, but a hole is more honourable than a patch	514
It's more difficult to maintain honour than to become prosperous	515
A man may live after losing his life but not after losing his honour	516
Honour is more precious than gold	517

Hope

Live horse and you'll get grass	518
Hope soothes the tired heart	519
Hope is the physician of each misery	520
Face the sun but turn your back to the storm	521
There's no flood that doesn't recede	522
Do not expect more than you deserve	523

God never sent a mouth without something
    with it   524

The dogs have not eaten up the end of the year yet   525

Good hope is better than a bad intention   526

There are fish in the tide as good as any that has
    been taken   527

There's fish in the sea better than was ever caught   528

In the end the improvement comes   529

The night and the day are as long as ever they
    were   530

Humility

The last place is worthy of the best loved   531

The heaviest ear of corn is the one that lowest
    bends its head   532

Humour

Good humour comes from the kitchen   533

Crying is not far away from laughter   534

Hunger

It's a good story that fills the belly   535

Hunger is a good sauce   536

The mountain is a good mustard   537

The hungry hound thinks not of her whelps   538

Sharp is the eye of the hungry person   539

A blessing does not fill the stomach   540

Idleness

Ignorance

Impossibility

Independence

Inequality

Initiative

A shut fist will not catch a hawk 554

Strike the ball when you get it on the hop 555

Strike while the iron is hot 556

The man without resourcefulness is no better
than a pig 557

Intelligence

A spur in the head is worth two on the heel 558

Involvement

In for a penny, in for a pound 559

You might as well be hung for a sheep as a lamb 560

An inch is as good as a mile 561

Irishman

An Irishman carries his heart in his hand 562

Put an Irishman on the spit and you'll find two
more to turn him 563

An Irishman is never at peace except when he's
fighting 564

The Irishman is impatient 565

Judgement

Justice

Kerry

Kindness

Kinship

Knowledge

Law

It's no joke going to law with the devil and the
court held in hell   588

Beyond the leap, beyond the law   589

A good word in court is better than a pound
in the purse   590

Neither break a law nor make one   591

The law does not apply to the blow that's not
struck   592

The lying man's witness is his wife   593

Laziness

Winter comes fast on the lazy   594

Cold in the shoulder makes the shins speckled   595
(see notes)

Long sleep makes a bare backside   596

It's only a worthless hen that fails to provide
for herself   597

The speckled shins of spring is the envious one
in Autumn   598

Laziness is a heavy burden   599

You'd be a good messenger to send for death   600

Pity the man who waits till the last day   601

Ye look for the ladle when the pot's in the fire   602

The long stitch of the lazy tailor   603

A slow messenger is the better for your going
to meet him   604

It's a bad bird that dirties its own nest   605

It's a bad hen that won't scratch herself   606

Leadership

After the chieftains fall, the fight seldom
    continues   607

Lies

As great a liar as the clock of Strabane   608

The lie often goes further than the truth   609

God does not like the lying tongue   610

Life

We live as long as we're let   611

You will live during the year for we were just
    talking of you   612

Life is sweet   613

Life is precious   614

People live in one another's shadows   615

Twenty years agrowing; twenty years at rest;
    twenty years declining; and twenty years when
    it doesn't matter whether you're there or not   616

Life is the true historian   617

Love

Live in my heart and pay no rent   618

If you love the mother, you love her brood   619

They won't fall in love with the man they don't see   620

When the sight leaves the eye, love leaves the heart   621

After the settlement (the dowry), comes the love   622

Love is blind to blemishes and faults   623

Love hides ignominy and evil   624

Love is no impartial judge   625

House without hound, cat, or child, house without
    love or affection   626

Love a woman or a child without their knowing it   627

To the raven her own chick is white   628

What is nearest the heart is usually nearest the lips   629

What is nearest the heart comes out   630

Love cools quickly   631

Love conceals ugliness, and hate sees a lot of
    faults   632

She who fills the heart, fills the eye   633

There's no love until there's a family   634

Absence makes the heart grow fond   635

Luck

It's better to be lucky than to be an early riser   636

A chance shot will not kill the devil   637

The man who has luck in the morning has luck in
    the afternoon   638

There's luck in sharing   639

It's better to be lucky than wise   640

A meeting in the sunlight is lucky, and a burying
    in the rain   641

The lucky person has only to be born   642

Luck seldom lasts   643

Manners

Marriage

It's a lonesome washing that there's not a (man's) shirt in   660

Marry a mountainy woman and you'll marry the mountain   661

She's a good woman, but she didn't take off her boots yet   662

The day you marry your wife you marry your children   663

The blanket is the warmer of being doubled   664

She burnt her coal and did not warm herself   665

He married money and got a woman with it   666

Marry in haste and be sorry at your leisure   667

Maturity

By age or ability you're no child   668

Meanness

What you give wouldn't blind the eye of a midge   669

As tight as tuppence in a market-woman's trashbag   670

If you give the loan of your britches, don't cut off the buttons   671

'Tis strange that the man who is so quick to find fault is himself so stingy about food   672

To come with one hand longer than the other   673

Nothing comes into a closed hand   674

Men

Some men are like bagpipes...they can't speak till their bellies are filled   675

Misfortune

Mother

Nature

You won't get from a cat but its skin	689
The lamb is a sheep in the long run	690
Its nature breaks out through the eyes of the cat	691
Let the tail go with the hide	692
A wild goose never laid a tame egg	693
What can you expect from a pig but a grunt	694
How could the apple be but like the apple tree	695
Nature is stronger than nurture	696
He got it from nature as the pig got the rooting in the ground	697
Often a cow does not take after its breed	698
What would a young cat do but eat mice?	699
Nature will come through the claws, and the hound will follow the hare	700
If you put a silk dress on a goat he is a goat still	701
Every bird as it is reared and the lark for the bog	702
What is in the marrow is hard to take out of the bone	703
The wood will renew the foliage it sheds	704
What will come from the briar but the berry	705
The hand goes only where the leg goes	706

Neatness

A handstaff of holly, a buailtin of hazel, a single sheaf and a clean floor *(see notes)*	707

Necessity

One who is without cows must be his own dog	708

Make necessity a virtue	709
Necessity accepts no law	710
A blind man can see his mouth	711
You never miss the water till the well has run dry	712

Nobility

A king's son is not nobler than his food (see also number 38)	713

Obedience

Keep your tongue in your jaw and your toe
in your pump   714

Obligation

Pity the man who has a stranger's spancel on him   715

Ownership

To every cow its calf; to every book its copy   716
(see notes)

Participation

Patience

Patriotism

Peace

Perception

Pity

Poetry

Possession

Poverty

No-one is ever poor who has the sight of his eyes
and the use of his feet   770

There is no tune without a penny   771

A poor man never yet lost his property   772

Poor is the church without music   773

A smoky cabin, a handful of spuds and a
flea-filled bed   774

Power

No stopping the force of a going wheel by hand   775

No forcing the sea   776

Presumption

Don't count your chickens before they are
hatched   777

Don't bless the fish till it gets to the land   778

Don't build the sty until the litter comes   779

Praise the ripe field not the green corn   780

Praise the ford when you have crossed it   781

You must empty a box before you fill it again   782

Pride

The pride of women and the pride of priests   783

It is difficult to soothe the proud   784

Pride comes before a fall   785

Pride feels no pain   786

Pride is the author of every sin   787

The jump of a cock on the dungheap   788

Procrastination

Promise

Proverbs

Prudence

Red-hair

If you meet a red-haired woman, you'll meet a
crowd   799

To be red-haired is better than to be without a
head   800

Repentance

To put off repentance is dangerous   801

It's better to be sorry and stay than to be sorry
and go away   802

Reputation

It's a small thing that outlives a man   803

Remember even if you lose all, keep your good
name for if you lose that you are worthless   804

Those who get the name of rising early may lie
all day   805

When a man gets his feet in lime he cannot
easily get rid of it   806

Revenge

No dealing with a revengeful man   807

Rogue

He was never good since the time a yard (of cloth)
made a coat for him   808

Don't mention him and a decent man in the
one day   809

A sly rogue is often in good dress	810
She would drink the cream and say the cat she had was an old rogue	811
The horse with the most scars is the one that highest kicks his rear	812

Rumour

The person who brings a story to you will take away two from you	813
A story without an author is not worth listening to	814
Leave the bad tale where you found it	815
There is no smoke without fire	816

(See also **Gossip**)

Scarcity

When all fruits fail welcome haws	817
When the fruit is scarcest, its taste is sweetest	818
We have a fine day more often than a kiln-cast	819

Seasons

A soft-dropping April brings milk to cows and sheep	820
Autumn days come quickly like the running of a hound on the moor	821
A misty winter brings a pleasant spring, a pleasant winter a misty spring	822
Many a sudden change takes place on a spring day	823
In winter the milk goes to the cow's horns	824

Secret

A secret is a weapon and a friend	825
It is no secret that is known to three	826
Fences (ditches) have ears	827
Don't tell your secret even to a fence	828
Woe to the man that entrusts his secrets to a ditch	829
The secret of an old woman scolding	830
If it's a secret, it's binding	831
Don't tell secrets to the children of your relatives	832

Self-Destruction

No tree but has rotten wood enough to burn it	833
A man may be his own ruin	834
A wedge from itself splits the oak tree	835
A man has often cut a rod to beat himself	836

Selfishness

It's for her own good that the cat purrs	837
His own wound is what everyone feels soonest	838
What is nearest the heart is nearest the mouth	839
He who is best to me is he who shall get the best share	840
The full stomach does not understand the empty one	841
The man who was dividing Ireland didn't leave himself last	842

Sense

Sense doesn't come before age	843

Separation

After the gathering comes the scattering	844

Shame

What would shame him would turn back a funeral	845
A fist full of gain and a village full of shame	846

Better is the trouble that follows death than the
trouble that follows shame   847

Shyness

Do not keep your tongue under your belt   848
A man is shy in another man's corner   849

Silence

A silent mouth is musical   850
The silent are often guilty   851
The silent mouth is sweet to hear   852
When wrathful words arise a closed mouth is
soothing   853
The stars make no noise   854
Little talk is easy to cure   855
A closed mouth.....a wise head   856
A silent mouth never did any harm   857

Strength

Strength is not enduring   858

Stupidity

Sending the goose on a message to the fox's den   859
Putting the fox to mind the geese   860
You didn't turn up when sense was being
distributed   861

Success

Suitability

Tact

Better sit beside him than in his place   867
A short visit is best and that not too often   868
The eye should be blind in the home of another   869
It's often a man's mouth broke his nose   870
Don't say everything you want to say lest you
    hear something you would not like to hear   871
Don't let your tongue cut your throat   872
See not what you see and hear not what you hear   873
Never speak to the feet while the head is alive   874
Don't rest your eyes beyond what is your own   875
It's bad manners to talk about ropes in the house
    of a man whose father was hanged   876

Talent

A greyhound finds food in its feet   877
The slow hound often has good qualities   878
The bird that can sing and won't sing should be
    made to sing   879
A cat between two houses, a rabbit between two
    holes, the two liveliest   879a

Talkativeness

Great talk and little action   880
Do not be talkative in an alehouse   881
You kissed the blarney stone   882

Thrift

Time

Treachery

Trouble

Trust

Truth

A man with a loud laugh makes truth itself seem folly	895
Truth is great and will win out	896
Even the truth may be bitter	897
There are two tellings to every story	898
Drunkenness and anger, 'tis said tell the truth	899
What I'm afraid to hear I'd better say first myself	900
Truth speaks even though the tongue were dead	901
You can keep away from the rogue, but you cannot keep yourself safe from the liar	902
Truth stands when everything else falls	903
It is no shame to tell the truth	904
Tell the truth and shame the devil	905

Understanding

The well-filled belly has little understanding of the empty	906
'Tis afterwards that everything is understood	907

Uselessness

It's a bad hound that's not worth the whistling	908
He knows how many grains to a bushel of wheat	909
He knows the price of everything and the value of nothing	910
He couldn't drag a herring off the coals	911
It's just a wisp in place of a brush	912

Value

One pair of good soles is worth two pairs of
    upper leathers   913

Without pressing too little or too hard, hold
    tight the reins for he's a fool who would not
    get value from a borrowed horse   914

It's not worth a cuckoo-spit   915

Better an idle house than a bad tenant   916

Vanity

Pity him who makes his opinion a certainty   917

He thinks that he himself is the very stone
    that was hurled at the castle   918

He dotes on his midden and thinks it the moon   919

Warning

That's a spoon ye'll sup sorrow with yet   920

Wastefulness

Wilful waste makes woeful want   921

Wealth

A shamefaced man seldom acquires wealth   922

The money-maker (profiteer) is never tired   923

The doorstep of a great house is slippery   924

There is misfortune only where there is wealth   925

Sweet is the voice of the man who has wealth   926

A hut is a palace to a poor man   927

A heavy purse makes a light heart   928

There's little value in the single cow   929

A man of one cow—a man of no cow   930

It's easy to knead when meal is at hand   931

Weather

Wind from the east is good for neither man nor
beast   932

A Kerry shower is of twenty-four hours   933

Better April showers than the breadth of the ocean
in gold   934

Welcome

Better for a man to have even a dog welcome
him than bark at him   935

Going in is not the same as coming out 936

A welcome is a debtor's face 937

Widow

What's all the world to a man when his wife is
a widow 938

Wisdom

A wise head keeps a shut mouth 939

Everyone is wise till he speaks 940

Food is no more important than wisdom 941

A contraction (in writing) is enough for a scholar 942

The beginning of wisdom is the fear of God 943

There's no wise man without a fault 944

He may die of wind but he'll never die of wisdom 945

You can't put a wise head on young shoulders 946

Wisdom is what makes a poor man a king,
a weak person powerful, a good generation
of a bad one, a foolish man reasonable 947

Though wisdom is good in the beginning, it is
better at the end 948

A little of anything isn't worth a pin; but a wee
bit of sense is worth a lot 949

No making of a wise man 950

Women

A dishonest woman can't be kept in and an
honest woman won't 951

There is no thing wickeder than a woman of
evil temper   952

A bad woman (wife) drinks a lot of her own bad
butter-milk   953

A foolish woman knows a foolish man's faults   954

A whistling woman and a crowing hen will bring
no luck to the house they are in   955

Beef to the heels like a Mullingar heifer   956

Eight lives for the men and nine for the women   957

Wherever there are women there's talking, and
wherever there's geese there's cackling   958

Irishwomen have a dispensation from the Pope
to wear the thick ends of their legs downwards   959

Women are shy and shame prevents them from
refusing a man   960

Everything dear is a woman's fancy   961

Like an Irish wolf she barks at her own shadow   962

She wipes the plate with the cat's tail   963

More hair than tit, like a mountain heifer   964

Women are stronger than men, they do not die
of wisdom   965

When the old woman is hard pressed, she has
to run   966

It's difficult to trust a woman   967

Man to the hills, woman to the shore   968

Beat a woman with a hammer and you'll have gold   969

'Tis as hard to see a woman cry, as a goose go
barefoot   970

'Where comes a cow,' the wise man lay down
(St Colmcille), 'there follows a woman, and
where comes a woman follows trouble'   971

Only a fool would prefer food to a woman   972

Don't be ever in a court or a castle without a
    woman to make your excuse   973

An excuse is nearer to a woman than her apron   974

There is nothing sharper than a woman's tongue   975

A woman without is she who has neither pipe nor
    child   976

The yellow praiseach (kale) of the fields that brings
    the Meath women to harm   977

A woman like a goose, a sharp pecking woman
A woman like a pig, a sleepy-headed woman
A woman like a sickle, a strong stubborn woman
A woman like a goat, a woman of rushing visits
A woman like a sheep, an affable friendly woman
A woman like a lamb, a quiet friendly woman   978

It is not the most beautiful woman who has the
    most sense   979

A woman can beat the devil   980

A shrew gets her wish but suffers in the getting   981

Work

Many a time the man with ten (cows) has
    overtaken the man with forty (cows)   982

Do it as if there was fire in your skin   983

The seeking for one thing will find another   984

Make your hay before the fine weather leaves you 985

Sow early and mow early   986

The early riser gets through his business but
    not through early rising   987

The slow horse reaches the mill   988

Making the beginning is one third of the work   989

The quiet pigs eat all the draff   990

The sweat of one's brow is what burns everyone   991

Everyone lays a burden on the willing horse 992

Every little makes a mickle 993

Speed and accuracy do not agree 994

Never put off tomorrow what you can do today 995

I'll go there tonight for evening is speedier than morning 996

The person of the greatest talk is the person of the least work 997

Be there with the day and be gone with the day 998

About evening a man is known 999

Long churning makes bad butter 1000

Scattering is easier than gathering 1001

The labour of the crow 1002

Put it on your shoulder and say it is not a burden 1003

It's no delay to stop to edge the tool 1004

The mason who strikes often is better than the one who strikes too hard 1005

It destroys the craft not to learn it 1006

The dog that's always on the go, is better than the one that's always curled up 1007

Handfulls make a load 1008

Don't go early or late to the well 1009

A good beginning is half the work 1010

Youth

Praise the young and they will make progress   1011
Many a shabby colt makes a fine horse   1012
The young shed many skins   1013
Youth likes to wander   1014
The growth of the gosling   1015
Youth cannot believe   1016

TRIADS

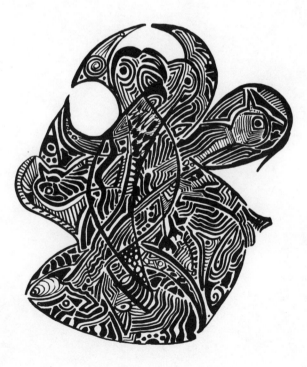

Three as good as

Three things as good as the best; dirty water to quench a fire, a frieze coat on a frosty day and black bread in famine time. 1017

Three things that are as good as things better than them; a wooden sword in a coward's hand, an ugly wife married to a blind man and poor clothes on a drunken man. 1018

Three best

Three best friends and three worst enemies; fire, wind and rain. 1019

Three best to have in plenty; sunshine, wisdom and generosity. 1020

Three best things to have a surplus of; money after paying the rent, seed after spring and friends at home. 1021

Three best invitations; come to mass, come and make secure and come to the mill. 1022

Three with the best sight; the eye of a blacksmith on a nail, the eye of a young girl at a contest and the eye of a priest on his parish. 1023

Three best small; a beehive, a sheep and a woman 1024

The three best sounds; the sound of the flail, the sound of the quern, the sound of the churn. 1024a

Three fortunes

The three fortunes of the cat; the housewife's forgetfulness, walking without a sound, and keen sight in darkness. 1025

Three fortunes of the lucky man; fences, vigilance and early rising.   1026

Three fortunes of the unlucky man; long visits to his neighbours, long morning sleep and bad fences.   1027

Three hardest

The three hardest to go through; a waterfall, a bog and a briary track.   1028

The three hardest to select; a Sunday woman, an autumn sheep and an old mare's foal.   1029

Three kinds

The three kinds of brain; brain as hard as stone, brain as receptive as wax and brain as unstable as flowing water.   1030

The three kinds of men; the worker, the pleasure-seeker and the boaster.   1031

The three kinds of men who fail to understand women; young men, old men and middle-aged men.   1032

The three kinds of men who rise earliest; the husband of a talkative wife, the man with a stolen white horse, and the man with a dirty tattered shirt.   1033

The three kinds of poor people; the man poor by the will of God, the man poor by his own will and the man poor even if he owned the world.   1034

The three kinds of women; the woman as shameless as a pig; the woman as unruly as a hen and the woman as gentle as a lamb.   1035

The three most

Three most bothersome things in the world;   1036
a thorn in the foot, a woman and a goat going
to the fair that will go anyway but the way you
want it.

The three most delightful things to see; a garden   1037
of white potatoes covered in blossom, a ship
under sail and a woman after giving birth.

The three most difficult to select; a woman,   1038
a scythe and a razor.

The three most difficult to teach; a mule, a pig   1039
and a woman.

The three most difficult to understand; the   1040
mind of a woman, the labour of the bees and
the ebb and flow of the tide.

The three most fortunate things a man ever had;   1041
a mare, a sow and a goose.

The three most nourishing foods; beef marrow,   1042
the flesh of a chicken, Scandinavian beer.

The three most pleasant things; a cat's kitten,   1043
a goat's kid and a young widow-woman.

The three most troubled eyes; the eye of a   1043a
blacksmith after the nail; the eye of a
chicken after the grain and the eye of a girl
seeking her sweetheart.

Three traits

Three traits of a bull; a bold walk, a strong   1044
neck and a hard forehead.

Three traits of a fox; a light step, a look to the   1045
front and a glance to each side of the road.

Three traits of a hare; a lively ear, a bright eye
and a quick run against the hill.   1046

Three traits of a woman; a broad bosom, a
slender waist and a short back.   1047

Three ugliest

The three ugliest things that are; a hairless,
mangy dog, a woman without flesh or blood,
and a deceitful, shameless girl.   1048

The three ugliest things of their own kind; a thin
red-haired woman, a thin yellow horse and
a thin white cow.   1049

Three useless

The three things useless when old; an old
schoolmaster, an old horse and an old soldier.   1050

Three things that are of little use; a trumpet and
no tongue, a button and no buttonhole and a
wolf without teeth.   1051

Three worst

The three worst departures; leaving mass before
it ends, leaving table without grace and
leaving your wife to go to another woman.   1052

The three worst endings; the last days of a noble
old lady, the last days of an old white horse
and the last days of an old schoolmaster.   1053

The three worst endings; a house burning; a ship
sinking and an old white horse dying.   1053a

The three worst pets; a pet priest, a pet beggar
and a pet pig.   1054

The three worst things to have in a house;   1055
a scolding wife, a smoky chimney and a leaky
roof.

The three worse things of all; small, soft potatoes,   1056
from that to an uncomfortable bed and to
sleep with a bad woman.

Three things

Three things that cannot be acquired; voice,   1057
generosity and poetry.

Three things that arrive unnoticed; rent, age and   1058
a beard.

Three things to beware of; the hoof of the horse,   1059
the horn of the bull and the smile of the Saxon.

Three things a man should not boast of; the size   1060
of his purse, the beauty of his wife and the
sweetness of his beer.

Three things bright at first, then dull and finally   1061
black; co-operation, a marriage alliance and
living in the one house.

Three things Christ never intended; a woman   1062
whistling, a hound howling and a hen crowing.

Three things that relate to drink; to drink it,   1063
to pay for it and to carry it.

Three things that fill a haggard; ambition,   1064
industry and constance vigilance.

Three good things to have; a clean shirt, a clean   1065
conscience and a guinea in the pocket.

Three disagreeable things at home; a scolding   1066
wife, a squalling child and a smoky chimney.

Three things that don't bear nursing; an old   1067
woman, a hen and a sheep.

Three things that are purposeless; throwing a
stone on a bend, giving advice to a wrathful
woman, talking to a head without sense. 1068

Three things that remain longest in a family;
fighting, red-hair and thieving. 1069

Three things that don't remain; a white cow,
a handsome woman and a house on a height. 1070

Three things that can never return; a Sunday
without mass, a day away from school and
a day away from work. 1071

Three things that won't have rest; a steep
waterfall, an otter, and a devil out of hell. 1072

Three things that never rust; a woman's tongue,
the shoes of a butcher's horse and charitable
peoples money. 1073

Three things that never rust; a sword, a spade
and a thought. 1074

Three things never seen; a blade's edge, wind
and love. 1075

Three sharpest things that are; a hound's tooth,
a thorn in the mud and a fool's word. 1076

The three sharpest things; a fool's word, a thorn
in the mud and a soft woollen thread that cuts
to the bone. 1077

Three things that survive for the shortest time;
a woman's association, the love of a mare for
her foal and fresh oaten bread. 1078

Three things swiftest in the sea; the seal, the ray
and the mackerel. 1079

Three things swiftest on land; the hound, the hare
and the fox. 1080

Three things that leave the shortest traces; a bird
on a branch, a ship on the sea and a man on
a woman. 1081

Three things that leave the longest traces; charcoal on wood, a chisel on a block of stone and a ploughshare on a furrow.   1082

Three things not to be trusted; a fine day in winter, the life of an old person or the word of an important man unless it's in writing.   1083

Three things not be trusted; a cow's horn, a dog's tooth and a horse's hoof.   1084

Three things of least value in any house; too many geese in a house without a lake, too many women in a house without wool to be spun, too many horses in a house without ploughing to be done.   1085

Three things that have little value; the head of a woodcock, the head of a goat and the head of a gurnet.   1086

Three things a man should not be without; a cat, a chimney and a housewife.   1087

Miscellaneous

Three parts of the body most easily hurt; the knee, the elbow and the eye.   1088

Three that do not clean their snouts; the farmer, the dog and the pig.   1089

Three coldest things that are; a hound's snout, a man's knee and a woman's breast.   1090

Three to whom it's little sense to pay a compliment; an old man, a bad man and a child.   1091

Three deaths that ought not be bemoaned; the death of a fat hog, the death of a thief and the death of a proud prince.   1092

Three the devil has without much trouble; the mason, the bailiff and the miller.   1093

Three enemies of the body; wind, smoke and fleas.   1094

Three errors relating to corn; to cut it green, to grind it damp and to eat it fresh.   1095

Three great evils; smallness of house, closeness of heart and shortage of food.   1096

Three with the sharpest eyes; a hawk on a tree, a fox in a glen, a young girl at a meeting.   1097

Three wholesome foods for the driver; the back of a herring, the belly of a salmon and the head of a thrush (moorhen).   1098

Three bad habits; drinking the glass, smoking the pipe and scattering the dew late at night.   1099

Three happiest in the world; the tailor, the piper and the goat.   1100

Three strokes that are keeping Ireland; the stroke of an axe on a block, of a hammer on an anvil and of a threshing flail in the center.   1101

Three jobs that must be done with vigour; rowing, hammering and measuring the ground with your fist (ie. using the sickle). 1102

Three kind acts unrequited; that done for an old man, for a wicked person or for a little child. 1103

Three sweetest melodies; the churning of butter, the plough ploughing and the mill grinding. 1104

Three oaths that money swore; that it did not care who would possess it, that it would stay but a while with any man and that it would not stay with any man but the man who loved it. 1105

Three pair that never agree; two married women in the same house, two cats with one mouse and two bachelors after the one young woman. 1106

Three places that cannot be avoided; the place of birth, the place of death and the place of burial. 1107

Three times it is most likely to rain; early on Friday, late on Saturday and on Sunday morning when it's time for first mass. 1108

Three greatest rushes; the rush of water, the rush of fire and the rush of falsehood. 1109

Three sauciest by nature; a ram, a bull and a tailor. 1110

Three skills of the hare; sharp turning, high jumping, and strong running against the hill. 1111

Three strongest forces; the force of fire, the force of water and the force of hatred. 1112

Three truths; sunrise, sunset and death. 1113

Three unluckiest things to meet first thing in the morning; a mad dog, a man who lent you money and a red-haired girl. 1114

Three virtues of the drunkard; a miserable morning, a dirty coat and an empty pocket. 1115

Three signs of an unfortunate man; going bail,   1115a
    intervening in disputes and giving evidence.

The three characteristics of the Fianna;   1115b
    purity of heart; strength of limb; and acting
    according to our word.

Four priests who are not greedy; four Frenchmen   1116
    who are not yellow (cowardly); four cobblers
    who don't tell lies; that's twelve not in this
    country.

Four things an Irishman should not trust;   1117
    a cow's horn, a horse's hoof, a dog's snarl
    and an Englishman's laugh. (Compare 1059)

The four fortunes of the cat; the housewife's   1118
    error; walking without care; no water in milk,
    and sight at night as well as by day.
    (Compare 1025)

Four hateful things: a worthless hound,   1119
    a slow horse, a chief without wisdom
    and a wife without children.

NOTES

Proverbs 50 & 707

The buailtin is the part of the flail that strikes the corn.

Proverb 51

Ciotog is the Irish word for a left-handed person; it often implies awkwardness. In this instance, however, the implication is one of cuteness or guile. Various superstitions have been associated with the ciotog—including suspicion of evil or treachery (Note the English word 'sinister', from the latin).

Proverb 55

The Irish word 'meitheal' means a team of workers (neighbours) assisting one another at turf-cutting or hay-making. The blacksmith usually had the largest meitheal in the parish since his work at the forge was of such importance to the community.

Proverb 60

'The Old Woman of Beare'—a legendary figure in Irish folklore and poetry. (See Padraic Pearse's poem, *Mise Eire*, and Austin Clarke's, *The Young Woman of Beare*).

Proverb 71

About 300 a.d. when Corman MacArt was High King of Ireland, ruling from Tara, a warrior army called the Fianna was formed under the leadership of Fionn MacCumhaill. Around the Fianna and its leader grew a great body of legend still popular today. Fionn himself was noted for his bravery and wisdom (he tasted the salmon of knowledge). The Fianna eventually became too powerful for the High King but were defeated at the battle of Gabhra and disbanded.

Proverb 203a

The word 'cess', according to P. W. Joyce, may mean a contraction of success, or a 'contribution'. He refers to its use in County Louth as meaning a quantity of corn in for threshing.

Proverb 271
   Lough Sheelin is a large lake in County Cavan

Proverb 441
   Used as a reply when you are reminded by someone of a
   favour he has granted you.

Proverb 595 & 598
   'Speckled' refers to the 'heat-spots' got on the shins from
   sitting too long and too close by the fire.

Proverb 716
   This proverb is King Diarmuid's famous judgement, given
   about 560 a.d., on the ownership of a manuscript copy
   made by St Colmcille of a manuscript belonging to St
   Finnian. It must be one of our first copyright laws.

INDEX

INDEX

119

INDEX

INDEX

INDEX

INDEX

INDEX

124

Books from Wolfhound Press

for YOUNG READERS: two titles by Liam O'Flaherty:

ALL THINGS COME OF AGE:
a rabbit story
ISBN 0 905473 08 6. Boards 22x15 illustrations by
Terence O'Connell; £1.50.

A sensitive, gently told story about nature and survival its cha-
acters are a baby rabbit. its mother a wicked-eyed weasel. A
beautiful and classic tale. full of the emotions. mystery. magic
and reality of nature.

THE TEST OF COURAGE
ISBN 0 905473 06 X. Boards 22x15 illustrations by
Terence O'Connell; £1.50.

This is one of Liam O'Flaherty's finest stories about children, and
is ideal reading for young people aged 8+. Michael O'Hara and
Peter Cooke, two young island boys set out for night's bream fish-
ing in a stolen curragh. In the darkness they drift, unawares. out
to sea . . .

The Wolfhound Book of Irish Poems for Young People
Selected by Bridie Quinn
& Seamus Cashman

A wide-ranging collection of
poems by Irish poets, selected for the young. A dual-
purpose book, for education
and for pleasure; for the
young person and for the ad-
ult poetry reader too.

'This book cannot be too
highly recommended . . . a
treasure and a treasury.
Irish Press

'Admirable in concept, selection and presentation . . . it
is also admirable value for in
addition to the 139 works it
embraces, it has explanatory
notes, brief biographies of the
poets, photographs and a number of excellent drawings . . .'
Irish Independent

192 pages; 35 drawings and
photos.

Liam O'Flaherty

THE WILDERNESS: a Novel

Written at the time when O'Flaherty produced some of his greatest short stories, and was influenced by the work of Dostoievsky, the characters of *The Wilderness* — like those of the Russian master — are all larger than life. As the story progresses through conflict, argument and visions, the growing tensions lead to the, perhaps, inevitably tragic final drama.

Irish Poetry After Yeats

SEVEN POETS

The purpose of this anthology is to present a meaningful representation of the works of seven poets who between them reflect the major aspects of Irish poetry after Yeats. By including for each poet a generous and carefully chosen selection of poems, the editor has provided a work that can be read with a sense of the poet's achievements. The seven poets represented are: Austin Clarke (1896-1974); Patrick Kavanagh (1905-67); Denis Devlin (1908-59); Richard Murphy (1927-   ); Thomas Kinsella (1928-   ); John Montague (1929-   ); Seamus Heaney (1939-   ).

Liam O'Flaherty

FAMINE

A NOVEL

'Much the best he has written and he will not find it easy to surpass... he strikes the centre of the target again and again with an astonishing certainty. The Famine is the

Liam O'Flaherty

THE ECSTASY OF ANGUS

"The ecstasy of Angus is a state of rapture, trance and frenzy — all at once."

The Ecstasy of Angus, Liam O'Flaherty's creation myth, is a marvellous fable, imaginative, exuberant — a fine example of the storyteller's art. The story takes place

Liam O'Flaherty

SKERRETT

Skerrett is a powerful and vigorous novel. Set in the western island of 'Nara' (the Aran Islands), it has been acclaimed as Liam O'Flaherty's best-written book.

THE PEDLAR'S REVENGE AND OTHER STORIES (1976)
21 short stories   Liam O'Flaherty   224 pages   £3.60.
"O'Flaherty's success ratio is abnormally high. This book is great value.
Sean O'Faolain's review *Irish Press*.

PADDY NO MORE: MODERN IRISH SHORT STORIES (1978)
edited by William Vorm   12 photographs   224 pages   £4.50.
18 stories by ten writers — all award winners — represent the very best c
our youngest generation of authors (Neil Jordan, Lucille Redmond, Micha
Foley, Desmond Hogan, John Morrow, Dermot Healy) and four establishe
writers, Juanita Casey, Francis Stuart, Eoghan O Tuairisc and John Montagu

IRISH MASTERS OF FANTASY (1979)
edited by Peter Tremayne   6 portraits and 6 drawings   224 pages   £5.5(
Stories by six of the giants of fantasy writing: Charles Maturin, Sheridan L
Fanu, Fitzjames O'Brien, Bram Stoker, M. P. Shiel and Lord Dunsany. Wit
introductory essays and brief biographies by the editor.

IRISH HISTORY & CULTURE (June 1979)
edited by Harold Orel   74 illustrations,   Maps   398 pages   £11.00.
A comprehensive introduction (advanced/reference) to the rich cultur
tradition of Ireland from earliest times to today. Most valuable, precis
accurate information — ranging from mythology to population figures — in
continuous lively narrative.

A LITERARY GUIDE TO IRELAND (June 1979)
Thomas & Susan Cahill   Photographs   400 pages   £8.50.
A lively tour of Ireland's literary landscapes — an introduction to th
literature as well as the places.

GRANUAILE: THE LIFE AND TIMES OF GRACE O'MALLEY
(c.1530-1603)   Ann Chambers (1979)   Illustrated   128 pages   £4.0
The story of Granuaile, searching for the real person behind the legend.

ART LEARNING & TEACHING (Sept. 1979)
Dermot Larkin, Carysfort T.T.C.   248 pages   photographs   £5.50.
A teacher's manual of learning situations for infants to sixth class primar
school; explanatory chapters; glossary. Designed on principles of a
education this will be invaluable to all primary schools (and a useful referenc
for art teachers at second level).

WOLFHOUND PRESS
68 Mountjoy Square, Dublin 1.